# It's Not Me, It's You.

Politically Incorrect, Brutal
Truths About Modern
Dating… And Why We
Date The Way We Do

By Patrick King
Dating Coach at
www.PatrickKingConsultin
g.com

As a show of appreciation to my readers,
I've put together a **FREE TRAINING VIDEO**
describing my TOP exercise for immediate
social and romantic confidence. Click over
to watch it now!

It's Not Me, It's You. Political Incorrect, Brutal Truths About Modern Dating… And Why We Date The Way We Do

Table of Contents

8. Men aren't as oblivious as you think.

9. We rarely prefer the cold, hard truth.

10. Nice or sweet just doesn't cut it.

11. Guys have to be "creepy" sometimes.

12. Men are irrational before sex; women are after.

13. People appease, they don't change.

14. You don't really have many dealbreakers.

15. Male and female shallowness is different but similar.

16. All guys are "douchebags".

17. Dating games have one goal.

18. Sometimes you can't overcome 'taste'.

19."The One" is a harmful concept.

20. Women need to make the first move.

21. All you know is what you <u>don't</u> want.

22. Silence is almost always "Thanks, but I'll pass."

23. If you care less, you have more power.

24. Beware the honeymoon period.

25. We shouldn't be asking "How can I make them like me?"

26. You deserve a mutual, 100% "Yes!"

27. Date a late bloomer.

28. You might have FOMO.

29. You really do want what you can't have.

30. You don't miss them, you miss the security they gave you.

31. Women and men each want what the other sex guards closely.

32. Nice guys (and girls) don't finish last, people pleasers do.

33. You use defense mechanisms more than you think.

34. Only three things predict a lasting relationship.

35. Women are perceptive, but not to negativity.

36. The absence of relationships early in life is damaging.

37. Chemistry is whoever's subtle hints you understand.

38. Unattractive guys have it okay; unattractive women have it the worst.

39. There is always a reacher and a settler in a relationship.

40. Breakups have a winner and loser.

Conclusion

*It's not you, it's me.*

Of course, that's always a lie isn't it? You might have some extenuating circumstances in your life, but if you just **liked** that person enough... you'd probably fight to hold onto them.

**It's never really us, it's them.**

We tell ourselves lies about dating and relationships so often that sometimes we don't even realize when we're doing it, or who it's supposed to benefit. If you want an indication of how much we tiptoe around ourselves, just recall the last conversation you had with a friend about their relationship woes.

*"He always takes so long to reply to me, even when we have set plans already!"*

*"She never refers to me as her boyfriend even though she's met my parents!"*

Even though they have justified these situations to themselves brilliantly, there seem to be pretty simple answers to them that they want to avoid. **What tough love advice do you wish you could tell your friends, just once, without fear of repercussion?**

How about some **real talk**? That's what this book is.

It's full of **brutal, unfiltered, and honest observations** about modern dating that directly answer so many of the questions we have on a daily basis. They create the backdrop and inform many of the choices we **think** we consciously make when we date.

They are **judgmental generalizations** that are almost always correct, despite being politically incorrect and borderline taboo to mention. They probably aren't for the faint of heart, but they are why we do the things we do when interacting with the opposite sex, for better or worse.

**Politically incorrect**? My definition of that is I'm simply saying what other people are thinking and are too polite to say.

I hope to provide a good amount of entertainment, juice, and *"Oh my God!"* moments in this book, but I also hope that those moments occasionally turn into introspection about your approach to dating and relationships.

Date with more clarity, effectiveness, and satisfaction when you understand the inner workings of what people think and say. Know exactly why you're thinking what you're thinking, and be able to read others with accuracy.

If not, you'll probably get a kick out of most of the chapters, so it's a pretty easy win-win scenario.

Modern dating is a mish mash of technology, traditional gender roles, and shifting expectations. Read on to see what that means for you.

1. "Just be yourself" is bad advice for a lot of people.

This is a personal favorite, hence its prominent placement in this book. It's one of the things that people are told going into dates or relationships: *"you'll be just fine if you just be yourself!"*

There might not be a bigger lie told on a daily basis in the sphere of dating and relationships. *Just being yourself* is terrible advice for most of us because of what it conveys to the listener and what it implies.

**First**, it tells the listener to not work on themselves, and that continued growth and self-development isn't necessary for people to like them. Beyond the obvious fallacy that people shouldn't continue to work on themselves, it also says that everyone is inherently attractive in some degree – that there's someone for everyone.

**That's just not true**. Look, if being yourself consists of loving Cheetohs and Pepsi, sitting in your underwear, and not filtering your thoughts, there may not be someone for you. Just being yourself just won't work. But that's okay, because there is a better version of you inside.

**Second**, it causes the listener to feel entitled to people accepting them without having to work on themselves. It's like putting a damaged vacuum cleaner out for sale and expecting people to buy it without questioning it or complaint. Why wouldn't you fix the vacuum cleaner, at least?

**Third**, none of us even follow this advice ourselves.

We're never 100% completely ourselves, and just assume that things will work out fine because of it. Like it or not, we all inherently play some games because we recognize what drives human and romantic attraction. Are you going to sit there and tell me you don't act differently on a date to try to impress someone? That brings us to my fourth point.

**Fourth**, telling people to just be themselves is often a **pity** statement designed to raise someone's self-esteem. Self=esteem is important, but the true purpose of the statement is almost never to be sound dating advice. If that's not what it's used for… then why would we even expect it to be helpful?

**Finally**, and I briefly touched upon this earlier, it obscures the most healthy and optimal approach to dating and growth in general – **strive to be the best version of yourself**!

That's really what "just be yourself" is code for – stay true to your identity… but realize that you can improve it and sometimes change it for the better.

Suppose you have two friends, **Angela and Ben**, who have just split up after being together for 10 months. They are equally attractive, and everyone remarked that they just "*looked good together.*"

Now fast forward to 2 months post-breakup. How do Angela and Ben's lives differ at this point?

**Ben** is working hard in the gym, and has turned his attention to his hobbies that he once enjoyed solo. He's looking forward to meeting new girls, and finally worked up the nerve to ask that cute barista for her phone number.

**Angela** is going on dates almost every night, and could get away with not having to grocery shop if she wanted. Many of her so-called male friends have shown interest, and a couple have asked her out.

Regardless of whether Angela wants to do this or actually participates, Angela's **opportunity** to do so illustrates the massive imbalance of how different the dating world is to men and women.

**Women are drowning, while men are on the verge of dehydration**.

As a result of a variety of societal expectations and archetypes, men feel pressure to take charge of courtship. However, they typically compete over the same women that everyone else does, so many women are enabled to sit back and **passively participate** in dating. They can be choosy, and **curation** is often their problem. Women often don't realize how difficult it can be for men and the odds they are facing.

This is best illustrated in the context of online dating, where it is easy to actually track percentages and numbers. Take Angela and Ben again. If you put them both on a dating website, Angela would likely get anywhere from 10-25 messages a day, while Ben would only get replies from 3-5/10 messages he sends out!

Dating is truly a women's market, but that's not without it's negatives, as I'll go over later.

Most of how men and women act differently within the context of dating can pretty much be explained by the gender imbalance. If women are in such high demand and men are competing with each other and unable to date as much as they want...

[Again, let's look through the spectrum of **online dating** to quantify this disparity easily.]

**Men**: Why is my reply rate so low? Because of the gender ratio imbalance. She has too many messages to reply to.

**Men**: Why does she have nothing in her profile? Because of the gender ratio imbalance. She gets messaged regardless of her profile completion.

**Men**: Why does she not even have the courtesy to reply to my message saying no thanks? Because of the gender ratio imbalance. She has too many messages to reply to.

**Women**: Why am I getting so many short, or copy and paste messages? Because of the gender ratio imbalance. Because guys don't get many replies in general, so they learn that it is a waste of time to craft thoughtful messages.

**Women**: Why do guys want to meet up so quickly? Because…. Well, you get it.

Men are spread thin and are aware that it's super competitive, so they often spend as little time as needed to interact with as many women as possible, which sometimes is the best gambit for them. It's truly a **numbers game**.

Women are so overwhelmed with attention and potential dates that they

don't have the time to reply to everyone –
their issue is curation.

How someone reacts to you is not
necessarily a reflection of their opinion on
you or their manners, it might simply be
tied to the skewed dating economy.

The drive to be in a relationship and have a significant other is universal. We all want to feel loved and taken care of.

But once a woman reaches her late 20's and early 30's, you tell me if the motivation changes at all! Guess what is at the forefront of the minds of many **women**?

Bingo. **Children**.

And it's a pressure they hear constantly from their family and friends. Facebook doesn't help either because at some point, it becomes just a place to showcase engagements, weddings, and births.

Women are driven by this pressure because they know that quite literally, they their uterus is a ticking time bomb. They only have so few years that they can have children safely, and sometimes this takes them into relationships that they have no business being in. **This is why women seek out relationships at some point.**

What about **men**? Men can have children well into senility, evidenced by the famous Charlie Chaplin fathering his youngest child in his 80's.

When it comes down to it, men are concerned about passing on their genes... but far more than that, men know that if they don't proactively seek out relationships, they run the risk of ending up alone! **This is why men seek out relationships at some point.**

On average, a relationship simply requires **x** amount of effort from a woman, and **10x** amount of effort from a man. This is why a man might end up in a relationship he doesn't belong in. Remember, men are dying of thirst, and sometimes they might just jump at the first sip of water, however toxic it might be for them. But if they don't want to end up alone, they must put in the work.

In a dating and relationship sense, everyone develops at different rates and speeds.

Some people might have lost their **virginity** at age 14, while others lost it at age 34.

Some people burn brightly and flame out, while others are late bloomers. Everyone carries some baggage with them at some point, and there's nothing shameful about that.

But there comes a time in everyone's dating and relationship journey when they are simply ready to **settle down**.

When we hit that mode, it's like we've hit the **marriage fast track**. We view each of our potential dates as potential life partners, dissecting how our lives will be with them and where we will live.

Say for someone, that mode hits when they turned 31. They just want to settle down now, and are tired of the dating games. They meet and fall in love with a stunning woman that seems to be on the same page as him, and they are to be married within the year.

So while he obviously loves her, would he have viewed her through the same scope if he had met her earlier or later in life, outside of that narrow "settling down" mode he was in? **Probably not**.

In this way, **relationships are primarily about timing**… with love and chemistry a close second.

Is that a jarring thought? Why do we suppose that so many young relationships – high school sweethearts and young marriages – break up? Sure, part of that is because they are barely formed individually, so it is inevitable that they grow and sometimes grow apart separately... But it's also because they aren't in the settling down phase yet! They still want to explore and live life on their own, and their current significant other just doesn't fit that context.

For some, settling down means exploring with someone else. For others, settling down means that they've explored alone sufficiently.

It doesn't really matter which one you are, just realize that the relationship you're in – they might not be the ideal love of your life, but they are the right one in the sense that they came into your life at the exact right moment! It doesn't mean you love them any less, just that the right timing played a role in your relationship as well as love.

6. Your situation is not unique, you're just too emotionally invested.

*"And then he just stopped texting me!"*

*"He's probably just not that into you."*

*"But he did X, and said Y last week!"*

*"He's probably just not that into you."*

*"Okay, but what about Z and buying me V?*

*"... are you hearing what I'm saying? Those don't change anything!"*

Let's face it, we've all done this before, and no matter what other people have said, we still had to learn tough lessons for ourselves.

**Here's the ugly truth**: your dating or relationship issue is **not** really that complex or unique.

Plenty of people have gone through it before, including most of your friends who you consult for advice. However, you just choose to impart a ton of special meaning and assumptions because you're too close to the situation     to be unbiased and objective.

The situation is probably as simple as $2 + 2 = 4$, but being too close makes you view the equation more like $AB(2x + 2y) = 4$, where A, B, X, and Y are all assumptions made from **over analysis and emotion**.

Since this book is all about dating real talk, here's the real talk.

He/she probably didn't get hit by a car to not reply to your text, they probably just aren't that into you. If he/she was hesitant about the next date, they probably just aren't that into you. If he/she "accidentally" referred to you as their sibling, **they probably just aren't that into you**.

There's definitely a pattern to the answers that we work hard to avoid, isn't there? We weave these elaborate stories for ourselves to avoid the terrible feeling of **rejection** and similar dread.

So next time you're faced with something like this, first stop and think what the **most obvious truth** is. It's probably in front of your face. Next, take a step back and ask yourself what you'd say to a friend that was in your situation? You might be outwardly supportive, but you know that the small details like A, B, X, and Y wouldn't matter to you very much.

It turns out that there are very **predictable patterns** when people lose interest or when things are going badly, and it only takes someone slightly less invested to see them.

I'm sure you've heard this before. *Love can be a choice. Love the one you're with. Love is hard, hard work. Love doesn't come easy. Just work to love them.*

I'm not really a fan of these. To me, if you constantly have to remind yourself of any of those statements, it's a harbinger of doom for your relationship.

I'm not saying that love and a relationship should be a breeze, or completely without bumps or conflict. But if you're aware that the love you're giving or receiving from someone is a choice, that already makes it so much **less meaningful**.

Making the choice to love someone is kind of like **accepting defeat**; you won't ever truly get those feelings yourself and you have to force them into you. You might not *like* your significant other all the time, but underlying respect and affection for them should always exist – your love for them as a person.

Choosing to love someone doesn't mean that the emotion of love actually manifests. What follows is closer to **appreciation**, not taking them for granted, and appeasement. Then eventually, it's becoming accustomed to someone, and settling into routine, habit, and security from and with them. This isn't how I would want my future significant other to describe how she feels about me.

So back to the title: it's not really a choice you want to have to make, because in an ideal world, or at least one where you aren't with someone you may not love, **it's a feeling you can't help**. You can't help cooing at a newborn kitten, and you should feel that uncontrollable urge and desire for your significant other.

Making that choice is similar to saying that *maybe* you want to be with them, and erring on the side of yes. It's a common story we tell ourselves, that might not be in our best interests.

Really. Most of us aren't.

More often than not, we'll see the hints that you are dropping, whether positive or negative.

Okay, there are some notable exceptions to the rule, such as when I didn't realize that a girl rubbing on my inner thigh at 2AM was as good as a green light as I was going to get... I blame youth on that one.

Anyway, you have to realize that 99% of relationships operate in **shades of grey**, and we rarely give out bright red **STOP!** or green **GO!** lights. That's the nature of the beast: the chase, and how we keep sexual tension and intrigue.

That being the case, guys get hints more often than you think – we're trained to look for them, and dissect them endlessly with our friends.

So why don't we act on them when sometimes we should? It's very simple.

The risk for a guy to be wrong about a hint is **huge, awkward, and potentially shameful**.
If we misread a sign of interest and make a move, congratulations. You've just soured a friendship for the immediate future, and made things very **weird**.
That's just the nice end of the spectrum.

So it's not obliviousness so much as a **defense mechanism** that prevents men from acting on the hints that you so diligently (yet subtly) send out. We know what the negative consequences can be if we're wrong, even when we think we're right, so we don't always take action.

It's the very same reason that **women** often feign obliviousness and ignorance when they know their male friend wants to have a relationship with them. Sometimes, things will just sort themselves out, and they don't want to make an awkward scene if they are actually wrong.

People are a collection of **hypocrisy**, especially when it comes to dating. They'll say one thing about what they want, then turn around the next minute to completely contradict it.

The biggest place this pops up is when people state that they are incredibly direct and straightforward when it comes to dating, and hate **playing games**. This of course transfers to the topic of rejection – they tell people directly when they're not interested and prefer the same for them.

This all sounds great in theory, but **they never really mean it**. There are a couple of levels of emotional resiliency and thick skin that need to be developed before people can adequately cope with this. By and large, the people that claim to be direct and straightforward (and make sure that you know it) do **not** possess this type of emotional hardness and some might say maturity.

The very fact that they feel that they have to posture in front of others probably indicates that they are more **insecure** than average.

They might feel that they have rejected people directly before without any problems. Letting someone else down in a direct way is a skill that can be practiced, and it doesn't take as big of an emotional toll after the initial guilt wears off. They might think that their tolerance for that type of confrontation dictates their emotional strength and how they themselves prefer to be rejected... But they'd be wrong.

It's a false assumption.

So what's the overall message in this chapter?

People are less comfortable with emotional confrontation and letdown than they let on. Shouldn't be a shocker, but don't be surprised if it runs opposite to how people like to view themselves.

And of course, don't call people out on it.

## 10. Nice or sweet just doesn't cut it.

This is probably a move we've all tried to pull, and it began from when we were but **children**. It just made sense then, so we went with it. Here's how it works.

You have a crush on little Bobby or Susie. You feel shy or weird about making a move on them or otherwise making your intentions known, so you don't. What you do is you act exceedingly nice or sweet to them, and hope that you get your **intentions** across that way.

What's more, you hope that this endears them to you. You attempt to become an **indispensable** part of their lives so that they sooner or later realize what's under their nose is the best thing out there.

Sounds like it's right out of a movie... probably because it is. **It's not reality** and it's not how people really get together.

What people want in a mate is **not** dictated by simply being nice and sweet. Sure, no one wants an asshole or bitch that refuses to pick them up from the airport because they're lazy. No one wants to be treated poorly, per se.

But what is **attractive** in the opposite sex is not bending over backwards for someone and just becoming a slave. It's actually a lot closer to the opposite. A sense of independence, self-worth, and self-respect.

It shows a sense of **security** that you just don't find in those who try to ply others with niceness and sweetness. As with many such issues, it's not a stretch to say that **insecurity** is at the root of it... but all the same, niceness alone doesn't entitle you to anything.

Think about it from this very simple perspective – how many other people can perform the same nice and sweet gestures that you do for that person? So once you remove them, what are you to that person? **Nothing special**, unless you work on making yourself special and worthy of that person's attention.

Much of dating is an attempt to make others like you, but it's completely the wrong approach. Make yourself someone that you would want to be with, and the rest usually takes care of itself.

**Creepy** is a loaded word, and guys are absolutely frightened by it. Many guys know that they can be labeled as creepy at any given moment, and it can drastically affect how they act on a date or otherwise.

But let's dissect the word for a second. What does creepiness actually mean, and why do women use it so often?

Creepiness is usually a word to indicate that woman just isn't attracted to a male, combined with **forward actions** from the male.

So being labeled a creep actually isn't something that men can ever control. Women always say that they like a strong, assertive man who takes control and is sometimes even dominant – sure, women love that if they are attracted to the man. Then they're not creepy.

But remember the definition of creepy? If it's true, it means that even if a man is assertive and confident, if the woman isn't attracted to him, he might get labeled creepy.

This can be incredibly **damaging** to men, because it then teaches them that they should be more passive with women and take fewer chances – which then turns cyclical, because we think that that's not something that women prefer.

How about the following example:

**Sexy man** from a bar finds out your address somehow and sends you a bouquet of flowers: charming, resourceful, and determined.

**Ugly, awkward man** does the same: creepy, borderline scary, and uncomfortable.

Ladies, you can't deny that this is at least 5% true.

This also speaks to the general theory that the more **attractive** you are, the higher **threshold** people will have for you to do whatever you want.

Sometimes the difference between charming and creepy is just **attractiveness**, but that underscores the point that men simply have to risk being creepy at times… because creepy isn't negative by itself, it just means that you're being assertive in your intentions.

If someone decides to label that creepy, then that has nothing to do with you… most of the time. If you find yourself calling in the middle of the night and hanging up immediately when they answer, you just might actually be creepy.

## 12. Men are irrational before sex; women are after.

This is a chapter that I almost think is self-explanatory with the title. You probably chuckled and nodded right when you read it.

**Men** act irrationally before sex because they are focused on getting **sex** from a woman. They act more irrational the closer they get to it, because they can smell it in the air (both literally and figuratively).

**Women** act irrationally after sex because they have just made themselves vulnerable, and they are now **emotionally invested** into a situation that they don't know the direction of.

**Generalizations, shmeneralizations.**

It's probably not as pronounced as I'm making it out to be, but it's still something to be very aware of in dealing with the opposite sex.

**Ladies**, if you feel that a gentleman may be likely to commit with you, and you are pre-sex with him, maybe you should think twice.

He might be in the habit of saying anything he knows that you want to hear in order to move the chains and get to one of his ultimate goals. The problem with this is however that sometimes **men don't even know** that they will lose interest after the fact – it's one of the ways that they are irrational when sex is involved.

Sex still represents a chase for them, and there are not many ways to tell whether a man just wants sex, or is in it for more at the beginning. You can't separate it because he will act in the same way for either goal.

And guys, if you feel secure that the lady you are with is going to be *"chill and cool"* after you have sex, you may want to think again if you want to get involved. She may think that she is going to be okay with a casual or sex-based relationship, but once physical intimacy enters the picture, sometimes her tune changes very quickly.

You could actually **remove sex from the equation** and make this chapter a slightly more general lesson – people will say one thing about themselves, but will end up **contradicting** themselves.

That's the nature of the beast when emotions, relationships, and human interaction are involved. Just don't judge others for it, because you do the same thing as well.

Remember the last fight that you had with a significant other? If it was a big one, it was probably about one of the **inherent traits** that one of you possess. Cleanliness, habits, attention, patience, financial responsibility, or something similar.

If it was a big fight, then there was a core conflict, and one of you promised and swore that you'd change, improve your habits and behaviors, and overall just make the situation better.

Predictably, you'd change for about **3 weeks**. And then?

**It all starts over again**. Sometimes you have to make the choice as to whether this is something you can live with, or if you should just cut your losses and run.

The vast majority of the time, people **don't** actually change for others. They are mostly incapable of it, and that's okay. The best they can do is alter their behavior in an act of appeasement to their significant others, and while that is important, it's also ephemeral and **ultimately temporary** though not for lack of trying or desire.

A lot of heartache and fertile years could be saved if we really just internalized this fact of life. People can't or don't change who they are at their cores the vast majority of the time. We all want to be with the **exception to the rule**, but that's statistically just not reasonable or possible.

What does this mean for your relationship? You have to try to suss out whether someone is trying to really change, or they are just appeasing you with token actions. The former is a far stronger motivation, but unfortunately it's not easy for people themselves to tell what is driving them – a desire to change, or a desire to avoid negative consequences from you.

And it's time for some introspection, and you'll see how difficult it is to tell whether a change can be sustained, or if it's just appeasement. No shame in either.

14. You don't really have many dealbreakers.

This is one of my favorite things to dispel, and if I had to explain why, it probably comes down to proving people wrong.

Everyone has purported **dealbreakers** – things that they feel that they could never accept in a relationship.

First of all, I'm never a fan of these because I feel that it enables people to focus on the wrong factors that make a successful relationship. Would you REALLY choose a guy that went to Harvard over a guy that went to a state school if you liked the state school guy more? Why is that even a factor?

Similarly, most dealbreakers that people think they have are misguided. What makes a successful relationship is the **day-to-day relationship** you have, not the resume version. A relationship is just a collection of **day-to-day moments** that fuse together to form a long-term goal, and focusing on dealbreakers and other requirements completely ignores this.

The best way to figure out if something is a real dealbreakers is to visualize the following hypothetical: **would this tear you apart if you had been dating someone for a year, and then you discovered the dealbreaker about them**?

For example, you discovered that they were a smoker after a year? Probably not a dealbreaker at that point, and thus not a real one. Just a **preference**.

But what about if you discovered that they didn't want any **children**, and you definitely did? That's an actual dealbreaker because it's literally something that you cannot accept if you feel strongly about children. And there's nothing wrong with that, it's just a matter of how you want your life to unfold and everyone is entitled to that.

So the requirements that you have for your future mate, what are they based on? Are they real dealbreakers or just preferences? Likely the latter.

## 15. Male and female shallowness is different but similar.

There are a lot of myths about male shallowness, and how males are fixated on physical beauty and fitness above all else.

I call bunk on this.

We are all shallow, and that's not a negative aspect of our nature. It's only when we focus on the shallow to our detriment and to the ignorance of other virtues that it becomes negative.

But let's assume for a second that men ARE actually very shallow about physical beauty.

That doesn't mean that they are shallower than women; women are just as shallow in other ways. Namely, women are shallow about the **providing capabilities and resumes** of the men they date.

Let's think about this in **caveman** terms.

**Gork (male)** wants to find a fertile female so he can pass on his genes effectively. The younger and more physical fit, the more fertile. So its hardwired into his mental systems to search for that. The more young and fit cavewomen he can find, the more progeny he can have and the more his gene pool spreads into the world.

**Banik (female)** doesn't necessarily want to spread her genes into the world, but she does recognize that she needs a provider for her and her offspring. She will seek those that can provide, and where physical strength and power provided in the past, **status and money provide now**. This is hardwired into her brain.

So who would blame males and females for their particular preferences, especially when there are so many **evolutionary advantages** to it? Even though we're not in an age where we can be picked off at any time by a saber-toothed tiger, physical beauty and the ability to provide are still valued quantities in society. Overwhelming physical beauty can compensate for mental shortcomings, and overwhelming power and money can compensate for physical shortcomings.

Look around next time you're in public. You know this to be true.

## 16. All guys are "douchebags".

Just like the word **creep**, the word douchebag is a word that's often overused by women. But there's actually a very simple explanation for why it keeps popping up when women describe men.

Women like attention from men they are attracted to, but not from those they aren't attracted to. (Duh)

Most women understandably complain about unwanted attention, and recommend that guys only ask out women who show actual interest to them.

But women, let's be real. You don't always give out any signs of interest, and if you do, they are short-lived, vague, subtle, and **safe**.

So when it comes to guys and dating, we essentially have to risk being presumptuous and invading your personal space to even play the game.

This will inevitably lead to awkward encounters, and you may think that I'm a douchebag for being a little persistent, I have to do this because there's just no other way for me to get close to women most of the time.

Women complain about unwanted advances, but every time I make a move on someone, I take the risk that it's unwanted because it does work sometimes.

This is the root of why women think the dating pool is full of so-called douchebags – if we encourage men to make the first move 100% of the time, but discourage being hit on by men that you aren't attracted to... this means that you have scared the nicer "non douchebag guys" out of the **pursuing dating pool**.

**Guess who's left**? Guys who don't care what women think, and will do what they were going to do anyway. There is sometimes a healthy overlap between this, and actual douchebags.

So women, do you want someone that is assertive and sweet? Gentle but strong? Any other set of contradictions? You can see the **internal struggle** for males in a nutshell.

Let's make a quick little list of the dating games that we all **instinctually** play, even though we are all "straightforward" and "sick of games."

We **delay texting** back immediately.

We pretend to be **busier** than we really are.

We make our weekends sound more awesome than they actually were.

We **avoid** people sometimes, even though we want to see them.

We don't tell people that we like them, or care about them even though we do.

What is the common thread for all of these games? They all serve to **manipulate your perceived availability**. In other words, they make you seem busier, scarcer, and generally like your life is more awesome than it is.

Then, they try to force the other person to act first out of a fear that the scarcity will prove too difficult to overcome, and put themselves out there first so you don't have to face the possibility of **rejection**. Devious!

This plays on the well-known truth of life that **we all want what we can't have**. So why don't people like to play games? They are usually described as dishonest, manipulative, and just sleazy. If you can't make someone like you by conventional means, then you didn't deserve them in the first place.

Except that's a **huge lie**. Is it dishonest or manipulative to simply **understand human psychology**, and take advantage of it? That would mean that every bit of sales and advertising is unethical simply because it utilizes an understanding of people to work.

I'm not condoning playing games with people that you are interested in, but it's undeniably effective and can often make the difference between a relationship or date and nothing.

Of course, the underlying theme is **perceived availability**, so my recommendation flows naturally from that.

Instead of spending all this time and effort cultivating an image of a busy person who is in high-demand and unavailable, that time is far better spent actually **being** that person.

Instead of plotting your text timelines and how to reply, actually **become** the person that is too busy to reply immediately, and only has a couple of days free a week. Easier said than done, and it's not the path of least resistance. But if you were interested in that, you wouldn't be reading this book.

What's your favorite kind of snack?

The correct answer, of course, is Oreos.

But that's to me, and only me, and no matter how **objectively superior** they are and how strongly I feel about it, not everyone will agree with me.

Okay, there's nothing mind-blowing about this. In the context of snacks, everyone obviously has their own tastes and opinions, and they are entitled to that. Objective standards don't matter, as taste and opinion are **inherently subjective**.

What about when we transfer this mentality to dating and relationships? What does that sound like?

It just means the following: even at your best, no matter how objectively attractive you may be, **you won't appeal to everyone**. Sometimes, you can't overcome people's tastes, and there is nothing wrong with that.

The key to focus on here is that it truly has nothing to do with you. You have no deficiencies, and no reason for your self-worth to be affected. If you're a big bite of **peanuts** and someone is **allergic** to peanuts, we don't fault either party in that case do we?

The lesson in this chapter is straightforward and simple. Sometimes you just can't convince someone to like you. And for that matter, is that something you want to have to debate someone about?

This is a lesson about learning to **cut losses**, and just knowing that your charms won't work on everyone. This will help you set **expectations** to reality, not be crushed when someone spurns your advances, and really keep your self-esteem intact.

The time spent focusing on how to win someone over (when in reality that may never happen) can be far better spent finding someone who nearly got childhood diabetes from stealing Oreos from her grandmother's cabinet – **a much better fit** with the same taste and opinion.

Yes, that's right. The One is a **harmful** concept, and it is also for the most part a **myth**.

It's almost as if we have been conditioned with unrealistic expectations purveyed by our **media**. No way, that doesn't sound like us...

The reason The One is a harmful concept is exactly because it represents an **unrealistic ideal**. That, combined with the fact that many people take it too literally means that a good portion of the population simply doesn't know what a good, healthy, normal relationship looks like.

The One encourages people to search for that perfect fit right at the outset, and ignores the reality that **couples grow closer together** through hard work, dedication, time, timing – any number of factors. That's why they fit so well together.

If we follow this train of thought, The One feeds a sense of dissatisfaction with any status quo that contains even a slight amount of displeasure – this is inevitable when you are searching for a perfect ideal that you believe truly exists. You are less likely to commit because you feel that you are settling for someone who isn't The One, not realizing that The One is The One because of a ton of **hard work and dedication**.

People imagine that when you meet The One, you click instantly, complete each other's sentences, and **everything is just easy**. Every day is cloud nine, and every issue is resolved like an episode of a schmaltzy sitcom.

You may click for the honeymoon period, but once that shiny veneer wears off, the daily snags of a relationship start mattering. This is where people's flaws start rearing their heads, and you start internally determining if you can actually live with them.

Good times will always be good, but **how low of bad times will you accept**?

The best definition of The One might just be based on flaws – if you can accept their flaws seamlessly and they yours, maybe that's the real key to your best partner.

If you want a sign of how oddly we are socialized and what expectations society has heaped on both men and women, look no further than telling one of your female friends to take action and ask out a guy that they like.

Ask her to take the first step, and she will likely exclaim "But I don't want to seem desperate!"

Well... personally, I fail to see the logical conclusion there.

Men are always expected to make the first move, as society has dictated. Okay.

Women naturally are then enabled to passively participate in dating, as men are the active parties. Okay.

But where does desperation come in when a woman chooses to make a move? Because they are going against generations-old rules that **both sexes kind of despise** anyway?

Find me a guy that says he enjoys being depended on to read women and make all of the initial moves, and I'll buy you a boat.

Find me a girl that says that she enjoys only having to pick from the men who show up on her doorstep, and I'll buy you a damned island.

So despite the fact that we don't even like these conventions, why do women use the word "desperate" to describe their dilemma? It's just a facet of unfamiliarity, and doing something that women aren't used to doing – **facing potential rejection**.

Men are far more used to the concept of rejection because it is inevitable in taking constant action.

Taking a step back, it's just so illogical to me for women to only passively participate in dating. It's like being at the best buffet in the world (incidentally, this is exactly what dating is) and not making a plate for yourself.

Instead, you're sitting at a table and only eating the food that people walk by you with. You restrict yourself unnecessarily, and miss out on the food that you really want... or the people that you actually would love to date, but can't because you'd risk appearing "desperate."

Some sports figure said that you miss 100% of the shots you take. Let that sink in.

Some people think they have dating all figured out after their first relationship. Those of us that have had more than a few just shake our heads and smile at the naiveté.

I think that's something we can all *smug* about. There is a **huge learning curve** in dating and relationships that we don't even begin to dent until we've experienced every emotion from elation to dejected ice cream-heartbreak.

However, at some point after we've run the gamut of emotions, we feel like we've *really* figured it out. We know what we want, what's good for us, and what will ultimately make us happy.

You've pre-emptively visualized your white picket fence (or leather and fur handcuffs) for the future, and know **exactly** what kind of partner fits in beside that.

But how do you know?

You don't. Let's face it – all we learn from our past relationships is what we don't want, and what doesn't mesh well with us either on a daily basis or in a long-term way.

All we know is what we **don't** want in our partners, and that does not mean that we simply want the opposite – that is **not** the same as what we want in a partner.

For example, if you dated a really passive person and hated it, that means you don't like dating passive people. That's it. It doesn't mean that you want and/or need someone that is extremely dominant – that's just an assumption that we make about ourselves all the time. And it's so silly!

So what do we want in our partners? Well, I'll get back to you when I figure that out. It's just not something that can or should be quantified, because then dating becomes about looking for a specific set of traits. That doesn't really make sense at the core, does it? It makes far more sense to start with people that you can fall in love with and have romantic chemistry with, and then see if they have those traits, or if you can live with them not having them.

Trait-hunting is one of the worst aspects of modern dating, and unfortunately it's not going away until many more marriages are "settle" marriages and wither slow deaths or end at age 40.

## 22. Silence is almost always "Thanks, but I'll pass."

You texted them the day after the date. No response.

Huh, maybe they just didn't see it. Maybe they forgot to reply. You recall they had friends coming from out of town.

You text them 2 days later. No response. *Oh my God, are they okay?! Wait, did they get hit by a car?!*

Sorry, no. They are just waiting for you to **get the hint** that they aren't into you enough to see or talk to you again, but they don't want to make things awkward by potentially causing a scene by confronting you directly about it.

These are the times we live in. If someone you know is attached to their phone (this is everyone), and you don't receive a text back in 2 days tops, the signs should be relatively clear.

Is this rude? Perhaps. But the alternative is dealing with one of those nasty conversations every month. Maybe even twice a month for some of us. That's just a lot of rejection to deal with in everyday life, so maybe it's not a bad thing to avoid.

Rude or not, this reflects a very big shift in **how we prefer to communicate**. This is emphasized by how many people are meeting through online dating as well. When we are behind screens, maybe we are at our most comfortable. And as any YouTube commenter knows, the more anonymous and faceless you are, more ruthless and cold you can be.

This chapter is but for the sole purpose to inform that people don't often the courtesy of a polite "no" these days. If you're waiting for that, it simply won't come 99% of the time. Instead, you'll get a deafening silence, even when you want to just politely say hi – it doesn't matter. So no, they didn't get hit by a car, and they didn't miraculously not see your message. It's the age of Facegooglezon. **Of course they saw it**. They just intentionally chose to not reply to it.

The best-case scenario here is that they reply to it extremely late, but you know what that indicates? It's not quite a "Thanks, but I'll pass" but it's pretty close to "Well, I'm bored and you were on the list."

**People will go to staggering lengths to appear nice and avoid awkwardness**.

This is a subconscious truth that we are all at least a little bit aware of.

If you are **highly invested** in a relationship – if you give too much, are the one who asks too much – then the amount of power you have in your relationship is relatively low. At best, you have the second most power (in a group of two).

The reason is simple. The more you care, the more everything in a relationship matters to you, and the more you'll care about making it work above all else. There is obvious value in this, but not *power* per se.

**Power** in this context is the ability to dictate actions and generally **act how you please** with someone.

So the more you care, the less power you have because you are too focused on the **relationship's priorities** to act how you please.

The **less** you care, the freer you are to act how you please because **your own priorities** are bigger issue to you.

Is this an unfair, unselfish, and somewhat malicious way to view relationships?

Absolutely, but that doesn't mean that it's not true.

**For example**, man goes on date with woman. Man really likes woman, but woman is still seeing another guy. Woman has more power because she is less invested and cares less about the man, and therefore has the freedom to do whatever she wants. Man however is constrained by his interest in the woman, and becoming exclusive with her starts dictating many of his actions.

Curiously, this **power differential** also causes the powerful party to become more attractive to the powerless party. Just think about the last time that you purposefully ignored someone in an effort to dissuade them from asking you out. Didn't it just make them come at your harder and hungrier?

The lesson here is only one of **awareness**. If you notice that you seem to be putting way more effort, time, and energy into someone than them into you, you've just become powerless. And no one finds a powerless person attractive.

The original title of this chapter was "Beware the **elongated** honeymoon period," but I obviously solved that problem with this first sentence.

Beware the normal, and **abridged** even, honeymoon period!

Luckily as time and relationships go by, and people mature from multiple experiences, we become more aware of this phenomenon... but not always. And much less so when we're involved in it.

The first six months (give or take a few months) of a relationship are always sparkling. **This is the honeymoon period**. In fact, it **better be** if your relationship is to stand a chance at all. If there is already trouble in paradise by month two, I've got a rude awakening for you: it doesn't get better with practice.

The first few months is just not representative of the real world. You live in a fantasy world where your partner is your sole priority. Other hobbies and priorities get pushed to the wayside, and you might even slow down at work.

The honeymoon period is driven **by novelty, infatuation, passion, sex, and degrees of obsession**. There's nothing wrong with this, and the honeymoon period can be the happiest times of people's lives.

The problem is that nothing in that list represents what drives a **long-term relationship**, and many people project their honeymoon period success into how successful their long-term relationships will be.

This is why I generally ignore any sweeping proclamations of "They are the one!" or "I just know we are such a good fit!" within the first few months of a new relationship. Of course you guys fit well together – you're so focused on the pleasure of simply being with each other that you sweep your issues under the rug for later. Nothing is addressed and no arguments are had.

It's tricky and hard to see through even if you're completely aware of the phenomenon. You can't deny the feelings that you have, but best practice dictates that you think about what you actually have once those feelings fade a little bit. Is there enough **substance** behind the infatuation and sex?

The honeymoon period is the impetus behind many a **summer fling**, long remembered in wistful tones because the relationship existed in a vacuum of pleasure.

As for the "elongated" part – honeymoon periods can be sneaky little buggers. Some can last an **unexpectedly long time**, which can make people think that this is how things will always be, or that they're out of the zone of danger.

Can they, and are you?

## 25. We shouldn't be asking "How can I make them like me?"

In the grand scheme of things, people waste a lot of time scheming about the opposite sex.

There are a couple of kinds of scheming. The first kind, is the **technical** kind. The nitty gritty. Do I text her back right now or do I wait? Where should I take her on the third date? When should I kiss her?

That kind of scheming is normal.

The second kind is what I would call **attraction scheming**. How can I make her like me? If I bring her flowers, will she see me as a potential boyfriend? Will brunch make her fall in love with me? Why doesn't she think of me that way?! If I bring him cookies, will he want to date me?

This kind of scheming is also normal, but somewhat **misdirected**.

It's fundamentally the wrong question to be asking.

Say you're going to a **job interview**. Do you ask yourself "How can I make them like me?" or "How can I be the type of person employers want to hire?" The latter is unquestionably more effective. To get a job, you must have requirements A, B, and C – D and E are bonuses. You can't really fool a hiring manager, so you just have to **make yourself** into that ideal candidate.

Why don't men think that about women? Instead of "How can I make her like me" shouldn't it be "How can I be the kind of guy that she likes?" The requirements might be a little more flexible than A, B, and C, but you still have to bring something to the table that they want.

You see, scheming can consume some people. But if they were to channel that mental bandwidth and energy into actually becoming the sort of person that is desirable by the opposite sex, they would be so much better for it.

It's a mentality that can be transferred to all areas of your life – instead of trying to conform to what you think someone wants, develop the best version of yourself that other people want. **Inbound versus outbound** marketing, so to speak.

So what are you bringing to the table for the opposite sex to be attracted to and fall in love with?

We're presented with a lot of choices in modern dating. Be it from technology, or just a heightened sense of freedom and anti-conservatism, many of us who didn't previously were unable to get the dates we wanted now can.

But within that freedom is many **shades of grey**. We go on dates that we can categorize as good and bad routinely, but most of them we just don't really have a comment on. They're "whatever" dates, and that probably reflects on how strongly you feel about that person.

The proposition of this chapter is clear and easy. If you don't feel the need to scream a huge "**YES**!" at the prospect of going out with someone, going out with someone again, or even just talking to someone... then **you're wasting your time**.

You should feel a huge screaming "YES!" at anyone you go out with. Anything less is just **a waste of your time**. If you feel that you have to hedge and actually justify to yourself why you're going out with someone, then you've got issues. *"But he/she's..."* Yes, but are you trying to convince us or yourself?

So if, thinking of the prospect of going out with someone, you're on the fence and just aren't sure that you even want to leave your pajamas that night, let me help you. That's as good as a "No."

In the same vein, you want anyone you go out to think a screaming "YES!" about you as well. How would you feel if someone had to drag themselves into their shoes to even meet you? You're just worth more than that, and you deserve someone that is truly excited to meet you.

And someone that thinks "YES!" about you is bound to receive a warmer and more affectionate response from you.

The more you date, the truer this rule becomes. You find out what you think you like, what you definitely don't like, and you just develop a sense for who you'll have chemistry with. After all, aren't you supposed to be learning from each person you date?

Late bloomers – the former nerds, choir kids, mathletes, and AP-test crushers.

They plodded along through adolescence and puberty, just focusing on what was in front of them and not necessarily extending themselves in social circumstances.
Maybe they were shy, or maybe they just preferred reading to social interaction. Hell, maybe they just had a bad case of teenage acne and needed a couple of years of medication to clear it up.

They're **goldmines**. (Of course, if you simply loved to read when you were younger, don't go patting yourself on the back just yet.)

**Late bloomer**; *noun*: a person who went through periods of growth, mostly of an external nature, such that their superficial appearance now matches their inner charm.

One of the first things that I do when I meet or date someone new is try to ferret out if they were a late bloomer, and I'll tell you why. Late bloomers have perspective and empathy that people who never had to struggle through anything possess.

Take someone that was the **prettiest girl** in school since they were a child. They know nothing different, and they literally live in a **different world** because of how they've always been treated. She hasn't had to develop many aspects of her personality because she could get by just fine from her looks.

Compare that to the life of a late bloomer – perhaps she was shy and didn't bother with makeup or fashion, and only broke out of her shell in college.

She understands **both sides of the coin**, insecurities, and why people act the way they do far better than the pretty golden child. She couldn't get by on her looks, so she went through the process and hardship of developing **qualities** that they wanted, such as a sharp sense of **humor**. There's a reason most of the most famous comedians are late bloomers, and aren't the most attractive lot.

And now, after the blooming process has caught up to her, she's actually charming and witty inside with a pretty exterior to boot. That's why I love late bloomers – they have **wonderful personalities as a side product of necessity**.

Actually, the **most** ideal person to date is actually a late bloomer who still isn't aware that they have bloomed. That way, you get someone who is amazing inside and out, and yet feels incredibly lucky to have you.

One of the running themes in this book is just how much easier it is to date and date around these days.

For most, this is great. People need a few dates, relationships, flings, etc. under their belt to truly make an informed decision about who they want to spend their life with. It just makes sense that you don't use a **sample size** of 1 or 2 to make that judgment call. Sorry **high school sweethearts**, this may be directed at you.

Of course, the ease of modern dating is a double-edged sword.

With so many available choices out there, and the ability to have literally 3 first dates a week, many of us have been afflicted with what I like to call **FOMO – the fear of missing out**.

FOMO happens when you go out with someone, and don't feel compelled to commit to them even if you really like them... because you fear you may be missing out on someone **better**. Someone **else**. Someone **different**. Someone **saucier**. Someone **smart** and **hotter**. The list goes on.

It's a perpetual meat market where we are always on the lookout for **the next best thing**, and nothing is ever good enough for us. It's why we "hangout" with people so much instead of go on actual "dates."

In some sense, this is completely logical. If we have a lot of opportunity and access, then why shouldn't be fish for the best of what we can obtain?

Unfortunately, we don't live in an emotionless vacuum, and we are dealing with other human beings. So instead of this approach being effective and efficient, it's a bit **cold and dismissive.**

Worst of all, what happens to the thought of committing to someone? It just goes out the window – **what if** you commit to someone, and then meet someone 'better' the very next day or next swipe? It's a bit **damaging** to those who seek out longer term relationships, in that the people they meet will be less inclined to do so.

FOMO is a normal byproduct of modern dating, just like cancer is a byproduct of essentially everything these days.

No matter how strongly we attempt to subvert **human nature**, she's a strong little bitch.

So many of her functions are useless and vestigial these days, they do more harm than good. For example, **allergies**. Allergies used to be nature's way of telling us to beware of something that wasn't healthy for us, but these days symptoms of allergies are the worst part about them.

How does human nature apply to dating? It's the **undeniable pull** we have to people and things that we can't have.

This might have served a purpose earlier in human existence, perhaps to desire more scarce food and lodging in a competitive, **Darwin-driven** survival of the fittest sense. In other words, maybe we wanted what we couldn't have because it meant we were more likely to survive if we obtained it.

But now? It just means we want people that are out of our reach, or that have rejected us.

Most of the time, this desire we have towards them has nothing to do with if we actually like them.

This is an easily confused distinction that has driven many a potential relationship into the gutter. One party will decide that they really want another party, and they will pursue for weeks or months.

Once they finally obtain them, there is a slight moment of panic when they realize that they were just intrigued by what they couldn't have, and **the chase and thrill of obtaining them**.

It's a quandary for both parties. How do you know if you're attracted to someone purely because of the chase, **how do you know** if someone wants you because you haven't given them much attention in the past... and how do you know if you like someone for who they actually are?

That's the essence of the thrill of the chase. There's a lot of sexual tension that hasn't been resolved, and you're not sure that it ever will be... but you definitely want a release from it.

30. You don't miss them, you miss the security they gave you.

The previous chapter talked a little bit about confused signals. Do you like someone because you like really like **them**, or because they are unavailable to you?

One of the greatest confused signals is what follows a breakup. Heartbreak, yearning, and loneliness, to be sure. A mash of negative feelings that lead to lowered self-esteem and self-worth.

But what are you really yearning about?

**Option 1**: Do you miss the little things about that person that made you fall in love with them? The way they used to call you their honeybear?

**Option 2**: Or is it a more general yearning of the loss of a sense of security and comfort? Combine that with general sense of loss, shock, rejection, loneliness, a sudden deprivation of intimacy that was available to you, and a massive change to your life's routines?

Which seems more likely to be affecting you post-breakup? Option 2 seems to be a bit more impactful, doesn't it?

This isn't to downplay or minimize the feelings and connection that you had with your significant other.

But this can be downright **empowering**. If you can internalize that the reasons that you are feeling so down post-breakup aren't actually related to the other person at all, that means a few things.

**First**, that you are not dependent on someone else for your happiness. **Second**, that they were not so special that you will never be able to reach those feelings again. **Third**, that your grief is just part of a natural process of loss. **Finally**, that being happy will be far easier than you think.

Remember the old saying "To get over someone, get under someone?" Turns out that whoever coined that was onto something – sharing a physically or emotionally intimate moment with someone soon post-breakup can **stem the feelings of loss** that ultimately contribute the most to your feelings of yearning.

Throughout my writings, I often allude to the fact that men are **less emotionally open**, **vulnerable, and perceptive**. Women are less sexually expressive, desiring, and open. Generally speaking, of course.

The annoying part about this is that there is a near-complete overlap between those suppressions and what each sex feels is lacking from their ideal relationships. Men want more sex, and women want more emotional intimacy.

Men are women aren't necessarily wired that differently. But they *are* brought up and socialized incredibly differently.

From childhood, men are taught to be stoic, tough, not show emotions, not cry, and to simply "man up" when a tough situation arises. If they aren't able to do so, it's a jab at their masculinity and very identity as a modern male. Emotional intimacy and vulnerability are **weaknesses** that must be hidden and covered up.

At the same time, they are encouraged to be virile conquerors of women. So it's no wonder that men often have issues being vulnerable, even to the woman in their life.
Likewise, women from birth have been taught to suppress their sexuality, **slut-shame**, preserve false modesty, downplay their libidos, and otherwise act the part of "the lady." They are encouraged to open up emotionally to their friends, and socialize with empathy and sympathy. They are caretakers and nurturers, damnit!

Of course there's a double standard here, but what else do we notice about how we are conditioned?

*The traits and attributes that men and women have been taught to desire the most is exactly what society has taught the other sex to suppress.*

No, this isn't a chapter about undoing years of gender role socialization.

Rather, it's about understanding exactly what you're up against when you ask your significant other to simply "want sex more" or "just open up."

It's going against built in defense mechanisms, upbringing, the years of potential ridicule and shaming from friends.

They will likely be amazingly out of their comfort zones, so you must cultivate a safe space for them to open up either sexually or emotionally.

Men complain about this all the time. They feel that after treating someone better than any of their friends do, that they are entitled to a relationship with a woman.

They essentially try to win women over with niceness and the satisfaction of their every whim. While this might be attractive to women for a limited time (though perhaps the wrong kind of woman you want to be with), this kind of people pleasing is always a doomed attempt to woo women.

Let's get this straight – women **love** nice guys. Who doesn't like to be treated well and get rides to the airport when necessary?

In a **fundamental misunderstanding** of what women want, many men blur the lines between being nice and people pleasing.

Here's what being a people pleaser looks like to a woman: *Don't they have better things to be doing? What kind of person does this? What is he compensating for?*

When people, not just women, sense that you are a people pleaser, we see someone that puts other people's values and priorities above their own. Some may view this as selfless, but it actually tends to **lower their value** in a subconscious manner.

We also instinctually know that people act that way because of **insecurities** of all flavors.

On a more general level, people seek to please because they are more interested in the approval of others than their own priorities. They need it.

On the dating level, people seek to please because they want to ensure that the women they are dating have no reason to leave... so they take the angle of attempting to fulfill their every desire in an attempt to keep them. Well, that's not a relationship, **that's just appeasement**. And it's no wonder that women aren't attracted to it!

When someone is dependent on you, you lose your own independence regardless of whether it is mutual or not. Suddenly you're wracked with feelings of obligation and guilt as opposed to attraction and respect... which aren't the reasons that you want someone to be spending time with you.

Oh, what are other traits of a people-pleaser? They don't often speak their mind because they don't want to rock the boat, they are sometimes too deferential, and they are not assertive. Doesn't sound like a laundry list of traits that women often say that they go after!

**Ladies**, don't think you get off scot-free here.

Plenty of women feel that their way into a man's heart is to bake for them, cook for them, and act more like their caretaker than their mate. This is the female version of a people pleaser, and she is borne out of insecurity of being alone.

Most people don't look at themselves as cowardly, especially in dating.

If you took an informal poll (as all of mine are), you would probably find that people classify themselves as too picky or too busy to date. "If they really liked someone, they would just go for it."

But those (too picky, too busy) are just two **socially acceptable defense mechanisms** – ways of making excuses so that they don't have to take action.

A defense mechanism in the realm of dating is anything that prevents you from having to **put yourself out there** for dating and ultimately the possibility of rejection.

Think that you don't use any? Ever say "I'm too picky," "I'm too busy," "She's not cute enough," "I need to lose weight first…"

Be honest, have you used those phrases to hold someone at bay, or not approach someone cute?

This is representative of the types of excuses that we often make for ourselves. It's a **carefully constructed façade** and defense mechanism to keep our egos and pride intact… in an arena (dating) where it is impossible to do so and succeed simultaneously.

The pattern is one of **avoidance**, and it's a feeling that we all innately know.

If we don't put ourselves out there, we lack the **opportunity for failure**! Our self-esteem and ego remains intact, because we all know that if that girl was hot you would have chatted her up and gotten her phone number easily... right?

We see this in all aspects of our lives, but the scariest one to get over is undoubtedly in the dating sphere, because a rejection there is essentially a rejection of *the essence of you*... sometimes a **tough pill to swallow**.

Defense mechanisms are a necessary evil to some extent. We can't be fully aware of all of our shortcomings on a daily basis – that would just be too demoralizing to live with. Some are healthy, even.

But it's a matter of making sure that the defense mechanisms are a crutch for you to avoid taking action in your life, and that they don't dictate your life.

What *truly* matters when you're evaluating whether your current squeeze is in it to win it... or destined to come up short?

In other words, what can you ask yourself to definitely answer if you should marry them?

Short answer: Nothing.

Long, realistic, and nuanced answer: If you're looking for a magic bullet on this topic, it simply doesn't exist.

Very rarely will you ever come across that singular "A-HA!" moment that's going to decide the rest of your life for you. You can feel free to chase that feeling, but sooner or later you might just realize that those feelings only exist in the worst of rom-coms. And come on, men never watch rom-coms.

## So what matters then?

Well, I can tell you what won't matter to you in 10 years, and thus shouldn't be a deciding factor in evaluating your mate: their alma mater, what car they drive, how they dress, how musical they are, how much they hike, how much they earn (to an extent), and what their favorite movies are. And so on. You're making a **60-year decision** here! How's that for perspective?

The moment you start wanting these things in your mate is the moment that you place expectations on them and how you envision your future unfolding. As I've learned time and time again, expectations can be one of the most damaging blows to any relationship... because they simply don't reflect reality.

There's a reason that dealbreakers often aren't dealbreakers once you're in a relationship with someone. If your day-to-day chemistry is there, you're simply going to make the rest work for you.

Now that we're operating in the same context, we can revisit the original question I posed before – what questions can you ask yourself to make that important decision about your main squeeze?

## Does she challenge you?

A relationship shouldn't be static, and if you find yourself talking about and doing the same things with your partner year after year, it's a sign that you might be stagnating both individually and within the relationship. You should motivate, inspire, and encourage each other to new heights both individually and for the relationship. If the most important relationship in your life doesn't do this, it doesn't bode well for you individually.

## Do you respect them?

I'm of the opinion that no one deserves respect unconditionally. As a result, people have to earn it, and the level of respect we have for people gradually increases or decreases according to various factors. Therefore, do you respect your partner's morals, values, goals, habits, and choices? Do you look down upon them, or realize that you don't always have to agree with their choices to respect them?

Sometimes I'm a bit crestfallen when I realize how often this question needs to be emphasized because it is such a vicious animal that pervades otherwise healthy relationships so often. Here's a question to demonstrate that it's probably snuck into your relationship from time to time as well – do you occasionally treat your co-workers better and with more respect than you treat your partner?

**Are they, or can they potentially be your best friend?**

I alluded to this earlier – relationships are actually mish-mashes of partnerships, friendships, companions, and lovers. And once the intoxicating lover sparks inevitably burn out, your relationship is all about the friendship you have with them. They should be your favorite person in the world to spend time with – independent of any sexual relationship. You should be each other's main emotional support system, and know and love both their strengths and flaws because that's what makes them them.

So next time you meet someone and start to disqualify them because they might not meet some the requirements of your arbitrary checklist... think twice about whether that is just a preference, or a true dealbreaker. It's probably not the latter.

Most women will tell you that they are far more **perceptive** than their male counterparts when it comes to reading people.

By and large, they're correct. Women as a general matter do have higher **emotional intelligence** than men, and are more **perceptive** to what other people are thinking and feeling.

...Except when it comes to **negative** hints, such as those surrounding **rejection**.

The reason that women aren't as perceptive to negative hints is almost too simple of a concept to believe is true, but here goes:

Let's go through the timeline of a **typical relationship**. Man meets woman and man makes almost all of the initial moves. He is the **aggressor** and takes the majority of leaps of faith required for a relationship to flourish.

Most relationships follow a **similar pattern**, which means that men are fairly accustomed to the possibility rejection when their ventures do not work out.

Rejection is mostly through careful avoidance and negative hints from the woman, and is rarely as direct as "I know what you're doing, and thanks but no thanks."

Women, because they are mostly pursued and (mostly) take a passive role in dating, just **do not see rejection much in their lives**. They're usually the ones doing the rejecting.

Therefore, they don't always know when they're looking at or hearing a negative hint or cue… because they haven't had much exposure to them to learn. And since they are usually fairly indirect, it is doubly hard to pick up on. It's as simple as that.

This leads to some women coming off as quite insistent and persistent because they can't read between the lines of what a man might be too nice to directly say. Men of course, are far worse at rejecting people than women because they simply don't do it that much. It works both ways.

For example, if a man wants to reject a woman, he might answer her slowly, ignore her hints at getting together, and always find reasons to postpone or cancel hangouts. To most men, this would be a bright RED FLAG, but the woman is **unused** to this as a tactic and keeps trying unaware.

Hey, if I hadn't ever seen a rhino before, I wouldn't expect to understand it either!

It's a strange thing to realize that some people live in **completely different worlds**

on account of how they've been treated
so very differently.

Let me first define what I mean by early –
I mean before your late 20's and early
30's.

If you don't have a significant, or at least
some kind of romantic relationship before
your late 20's and early 30's, you may be
in for a surprise when you finally get into
one.

You see, you may think you have a
reasonable expectation of what a realistic
relationship is. But you are probably
**wrong**.

You'll have spent years being
indoctrinated by the **romantic fairytale
complex** that is unavoidable in this day

and age. You'll have spent years adding to the internal **laundry list** of requirements that you think you need in a partner, not knowing the difference between **realistic** and **fantastical**. You'll have spent years imagining what your relationship will look like, based on the good and bad ones you've seen over the years.

Most importantly, you'll have spent years conceptualizing what a healthy and realistic relationship is... and this concept will be terribly skewed and unrealistic.

That's what happens when you have nothing to base your expectations on — they soar ever **higher** because you aren't aware of reality and all the normal hardships that follow.

You've probably seen it in your friends that haven't dated much. They classify themselves as **eminently picky**, and that's true to some extent. They've created expectations so high and unrealistic for their mates that they are picky to a fault. They don't see anyone good enough, or capable of fulfilling the relationship that they've conceptualized in their head. Anyone that falls short is simply settling to them.

The sad part about their expectations is that they are very **one-sided** – they want many things out of a potential partner, but they probably aren't quite up to snuff with someone that embodies those traits. In other words, they won't attract the people that they want.

There's a reason that these friends just seem to remain single year in and year out, and it has much to do with the fact that they never quite **learned firsthand** that relationships aren't about **perfection**.

Romantic chemistry is one of the most sought-after things in the world... yet the harder you try to create it, the harder it is to come by. When you try too hard, you end up self-sabotaging.

But this underscores a very important aspect about **romantic chemistry** – it must be **natural**. It can **only** be natural.

It can't really be manufactured. It can be faked and manipulated for a little while, but it will fade relatively quickly if there isn't any **substantive** connection beneath the fakeness.

Romantic chemistry is defined in many different ways, but it really boils down to one aspect – you are just on the **same wavelength** as the other person. This is something that can only exist if you actually **are** on that same wavelength.

You can finish each other's sentences, and you know what they are trying to say right as they start to say it. You pick up on the unspoken messages that show through their body language, quirks, broken phrases, and implications. You understand their humor without them ever having to explain a joke. You get their **subtle hints** about what they think and what they are saying.

Imagine what this flowing conversation and connected interaction looks like to a bystander. Add in some light physical touching, strong eye contact, and smiling? Looks like **sparks** to me.

Chemistry is something that just exists between two people on account of how similarly they think. No, not about abortion and the death penalty – how they **navigate the world and perceive things**.

We all have favorite fictional characters (in television or literature) that we feel like we would be amazing friends with. Sometimes this is because we admire them for their courage, but mostly, it's because they are similar to us, and we feel like they would understand our **patterns of thinking**.

So when you view chemistry through this lens, it becomes apparent and inevitable that you cannot charm anyone that you want. But, if this person doesn't pick up on your humor, subtle hints, and inner processes... then who cares?

For all this talk about the **skewed gender economy of dating**, it's not always the men that get the short end of the stick.

If you'll recall, I talk about the skewed gender economy of dating at the beginning of the book. Men have been socially conditioned to be the **aggressors** in pursuing romantic relationships, which allows many women to passively participate in dating. In addition, the majority of the men fight over a relatively small percentage of women, which further enables women to sit back and literally have their choice of the pursuers.

Men lose sometimes because it's literally a **competition**, but they always have the option to keep pursuing other women. They may not get the ones that they had their sights set on or that may have been 'out of their league,' but if they pursue enough and capitalize on the **numbers game approach to dating**, they will eventually find someone.

Yes, even the most unattractive of men.

This is because women are far less shallow when it comes to physical attractiveness, and instead focus on shallow aspects of a man's ability to provide. This is the reason that gold-diggers are a very real thing. Think about how many old, obese men are with young pretty little things. Men can compensate in many ways to overcome their physical flaws.

So what about unattractive women? Well, they don't have guys fighting over them. Because men focus more on physical shallowness, they get overlooked constantly and sometimes **outright ignored**.

If they're lucky, they might get inquiries from time to time, but they're never anyone's first choice. They're always someone's **backup**.

Unattractive men can compensate with traits and qualities that women covet more than physical attractiveness. But an unattractive woman lacks what men covet the most in a mate – at least initially. The problem is however if they can't get past that initial superficial **gatekeeper**, their other amazing qualities won't really matter.

So as much as men can bemoan the fact that women don't give them the time of day, they're only talking about a subset of women that every other man is pursuing. They always have other options, and they can be attractive to women in many ways.

Unattractive women simply don't get any attention from any men, and they aren't accustomed to being the pursuer... so where does that leave them? In the worst situation.

Maybe this is familiar to you because it was hotly debated on the television show How I Met Your Mother – in every almost every relationship, there is a **reacher and a settler**.

A **reacher** is the person in a relationship that feels like they got incredibly lucky with their partner, and that their partner might even be out of their league.

A **settler** is the person in a relationship that feels like they are dating slightly below them, and that they could actually do better in one or a few aspects.

It doesn't mean that their relationship is doomed or headed to divorce. We all feel like this from time to time, and that doesn't mean we want to find someone better constantly. It's a natural thing and is perfectly acceptable in a realistic and healthy relationship...

**If those roles change hands and reverse every occasionally**. Every week, month, or year depending on a couple's dynamic.

That's how people stay engaged and how a relationship continues to thrive, even when you don't necessarily feel like you want to remain with your significant other.
It's a matter of recognizing that sometimes the **mundane daily routine** takes the mystique and attraction out of your significant other.

You begin to forget why you felt so strongly about them in the first place, and your eye begins wandering over to **greener** pastures and people and relationships that look better because you don't know the intimate details. You feel like you're **settling**.

Then your significant other makes a great joke, stands up for you, gets a job promotion, or something to reinforce your original feelings for them. You're over the moon and you feel a reignited fire for them that makes you remember why you fell in love with them. You feel like they've reached heights that you never could. You feel like you're **reaching**.

The truth is that **we aren't always 100% in love with our partners**. That's reality, and as long as the **pendulum swings** back to the love side as much as it does the not in love side, that's as good a balance as you can ask for.

Breakups are never easy, whether you are the dumper or the dumpee. There is always an emotional toll, even if you feel like you've escaped a jail of a relationship.

If you are the **dumped**, the emotional toll is clear.

You've had the rug pulled from under you. You may even have been blindsided, and the sudden loss of security, comfort, and a future that you envisioned can put people into states of shock and mourning. In fact, people who go through breakups often go through the same **stages of grief** and as those who have lost loved ones. If you can't relate to this paragraph, then I'm happy for you because you haven't experienced the lowest of lows... but also slightly sad because that's a major tool growth.

If you are the **dumpee**, the toll is a bit more obscured.

You know that you are going to hurt someone. You know that you have the potential to ruin someone's life for the immediate future and cause them to reconsider everything they thought they knew. There's massive guilt... and the dumpee also feels a sense of loss and inevitable **buyer's remorse**. The dumped literally has no choice in the matter, but the dumpee's privilege of choice in ending the relationship leads them to continually think "what if" and "did I do the right thing?" It's mental torture.

So if breakups are a painful event for both parties, how is there a winner or a loser? Well, just ask a friend who is recently single this question: *would you feel good if your ex got into another relationship before you, or would you feel better if you got into one first?*

That's what decides who wins or loses the breakup.

This is the source of many people's pain and frustration, even after they are long over their ex. They still don't want to lose the so-called race of getting into another relationship because they feel that it diminishes their emotional impact on their ex.

If she gets into another relationship so soon, did I mean anything to her at all?

And other similar troubling thoughts.

Unfortunately, many people **confuse this pain for feelings that are still present for their ex**. Turns out that we always want what we can't have, so this understandably causes trouble.

The next time one of your friends comes to you with a problem that you don't feel like listening to for the 50<sup>th</sup> time, just point them to this book. A strong hint towards a couple of chapters, perhaps.

If you've learned anything from this book, maybe it's just that people don't always have the strongest intuition about themselves. We can see others far more clearly, even the difficult lessons that we refuse to apply to ourselves.

But who's going to tell you the hard, brutal truths that you don't like hearing but need? Probably not your friends. Tough love is a limited currency, and friends don't have much of it.

Here's hoping that this book has been an eye-opening foray into how people really think about dating, for better or worse.


Sincerely,

Patrick King
Dating and Social Skills Coach
www.PatrickKingConsulting.com

P.S. If you enjoyed this book, please don't be shy and drop me a line, leave a review, or both! I love reading feedback, and reviews are the lifeblood of Kindle books, so they are always welcome and greatly appreciated.

**Other books by Patrick King include:**

CHATTER: Small Talk, Charisma, and How to Talk to Anyone
http://www.amazon.com/dp/B00J5HH2Y6

MAGNETIC: How to Impress, Connect, and Influence
http://www.amazon.com/dp/B00ON8WJKY

51963027R00078

Made in the USA
Lexington, KY
11 May 2016